GUIDE TO GHOSTS AND HAUNTINGS

Poltergeists

Craig E. Blohm

San Diego, CA

© 2025 ReferencePoint Press, Inc.
Printed in the United States

For more information, contact:
ReferencePoint Press, Inc.
PO Box 27779
San Diego, CA 92198
www.ReferencePointPress.com

ALL RIGHTS RESERVED.
No part of this work covered by the copyright hereon may be reproduced or used in any form or by any means—graphic, electronic, or mechanical, including photocopying, recording, taping, web distribution, or information storage retrieval systems—without the written permission of the publisher.

LIBRARY OF CONGRESS CATALOGING-IN-PUBLICATION DATA

Names: Blohm, Craig E., 1948- author.
Title: Poltergeists / by Craig E. Blohm.
Description: San Diego, CA : ReferencePoint Press, Inc., 2025. | Series: Guide to ghosts and hauntings | Includes bibliographical references and index. | Audience term: Children
Identifiers: LCCN 2024035121 (print) | LCCN 2024035122 (ebook) | ISBN 9781678209988 (library binding) | ISBN 9781678209995 (ebook)
Subjects: LCSH: Poltergeists--Juvenile literature.
Classification: LCC BF1483 .B56 2025 (print) | LCC BF1483 (ebook) | DDC 133.1/42--dc23/eng/20240910
LC record available at https://lccn.loc.gov/2024035121
LC ebook record available at https://lccn.loc.gov/2024035122

Spirits and the Spirit World: What People Believe   4

Introduction   5
Noisy Spirits

Chapter One   8
Perturbed by Poltergeists

Chapter Two   18
Mischievous Poltergeists

Chapter Three   28
Dangerous Poltergeists

Chapter Four   38
Seeking the Truth

Chapter Five   49
Poltergeists: Real or Unreal?

Source Notes	58
For Further Research	60
Index	62
Picture Credits	64
About the Author	64

SPIRITS AND THE SPIRIT WORLD: WHAT PEOPLE BELIEVE

Belief in Spirits

% of US adults who say . . .

Statement	%
They believe people have a soul or spirit in addition to their physical body	83%
There is something spiritual beyond the natural world, even if we cannot see it	81%
There are some things that science cannot possibly explain	74%
They have had a sudden feeling of connection with something from beyond this world	45%
They have a strong feeling that someone who has passed away was communicating with them from beyond this world	38%
They believe spirits or unseen spiritual forces exist and they have personally encountered one	30%

Communication Between the Living and the Dead

% of US adults who believe it is definitely or probably true that people who have died can . . .

Statement	%
Be united with other loved ones who have already died	57%
Provide assistance, protection, or guidance to the living	46%
Be aware of things going on among the living	44%
Communicate with the living	42%
Be reincarnated	27%
Harm the living	18%

Hearing from the World Beyond

% of US adults who say they . . .

Statement	%
Have had a sudden feeling of connection with someone from beyond this world	45%
Have had a strong feeling that someone who has passed away was communicating with them from beyond this world	38%
Believe spirits or unseen spiritual forces exist and they have personally encountered one	30%

Noisy Spirits

Fourteen-year-old Jason Cobb of Savannah, Georgia, was having trouble sleeping in the antique bed his father bought for him for Christmas. Although Jason was pleased with his new gift, odd things had begun to occur from the first night it was placed in his bedroom. He had the eerie feeling that someone—or something—was leaning on his pillow and breathing cold air down his neck. One morning he awoke to discover that a framed photograph and several other objects had been moved from their normal places. On numerous occasions, many of Jason's toys had been relocated, leading Jason's father, Al, to believe these happenings were caused by the spirit of a deceased child. "Casper, is that you?" he uttered in frustration, invoking the name of a famous fictional child ghost. "Are you a little six-year-old boy who has been playing with my son's toys?"[1]

> "Casper, is that you? Are you a little six-year-old boy who has been playing with my son's toys?"[1]
>
> —Al Cobb, addressing a poltergeist

Jason was spooked and spent several weeks sleeping in another room. When he decided to return to his own room, the strange antics began once more. This time Jason reported that a decorative terra-cotta figure flew from its place on a wall, nearly hitting him as it sailed across the room. Such spooky activity soon spread to the rest of the house, with kitchen cabinets opening by themselves and furniture moving although untouched.

After experiencing many other disturbing incidents, the Cobb family finally had enough. They sold the bed, but not before warning the buyers about the mysterious events connected to it. The new owners reported similar odd events taking place in their house. Before long, the bed changed hands once more. But in the Cobb household, Jason was finally able to get a good night's sleep.

Ghostly Commotion

Believers in the paranormal would consider the eerie experiences that disrupted the Cobb family to be classic examples of the mischievous behavior of poltergeists, or noisy ghosts. While ghosts are usually thought of as entities that appear and disappear without leaving a trace, poltergeists actively announce their presence by making noises and moving objects. The sudden occurrence of knocking or rapping sounds, things moving on their own, and physical contact with unseen entities can frighten even the most levelheaded person. But more disconcerting is the idea that, although rare, some behavior attributed to poltergeists can destroy property or cause actual physical injury.

Stories of such strange and unexplained incidents have been told as far back as ancient times. The term *poltergeist* was first coined in Germany during the sixteenth century to describe this bizarre activity. At a time when religion had more influence on European society than scientific inquiry did, spirits or demons were thought to be the cause of any number of mischievous doings. By the nineteenth century, many Americans had come to embrace a supernatural origin of many unexplained (and unexplainable) events. A movement called Spiritualism arose. Its adherents believed that the spirits of the dead could communicate with the living. People who described themselves as Spiritualists held séances in which they sought to connect with those spirits. Spiritualism became both a serious practice as well as a popular source of entertainment.

A Ghost or Something Else?

The term *poltergeist* is a combination of two German words: *poltern*, which means rumble or noise, and *geist*, which is a ghost or spirit. Although the word *ghost* comes from *poltergeist*, a controversy arose as to whether such entities were ghosts at all. Ghosts have long been considered by believers to be the restless spirits, or souls, of the departed. They may be visible, but they do not physically affect the world around them. Paranormal researchers who study poltergeists today, however, believe that they are not ghosts but rather a form of kinetic energy produced unconsciously by a living person. Most often the source is believed to

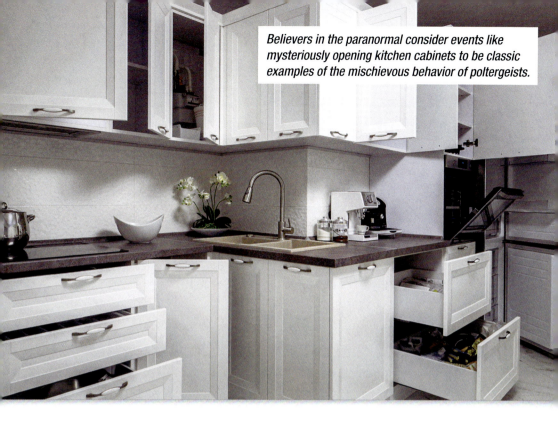
Believers in the paranormal consider events like mysteriously opening kitchen cabinets to be classic examples of the mischievous behavior of poltergeists.

be a child or teen because poltergeist activity tends to occur in the presence of a young person.

As with other strange phenomena, such as unidentified flying objects (UFOs), extrasensory perception (ESP), and Bigfoot, believers and skeptics have their own theories about poltergeists. For believers, poltergeists are proof that paranormal entities exist and can make themselves known by manipulating physical objects. Skeptics point to a lack of scientific evidence and attribute poltergeists to psychological anomalies, electrical brain activity, natural phenomena, or just plain hoaxes. Organizations that study paranormal phenomena have also taken sides. For example, the Society for Psychical Research (SPR) in England usually suggests that such events are real, whereas the Center for Scientific Inquiry in the United States is generally more skeptical of claims of paranormal activity.

Although both sides have their supporters, the reality of poltergeists continues to be debated. Whether they are ghosts, another kind of paranormal entity, or the inner workings of the human mind, poltergeists continue to fascinate, frighten, and often bewilder witnesses and researchers alike.

Perturbed by Poltergeists

In a modest brick house in Coventry, England, a bedroom on the upper floor was decorated with pink walls and furniture, creating a pleasant retreat for a typical preteen girl. But when the Manning family moved into the home in September 2011, eleven-year-old Elle grew so afraid of it that she began sleeping in another part of the house. The reason for her fear can be seen in a startling YouTube video of the bedroom shot by Elle's mother, Lisa. "I couldn't believe it when I played the tape back," Lisa said. "It sent chills up my spine."[2] The eerie video shows the bedroom's closet door suddenly swinging open and a chair sliding across the floor, both untouched by a human hand or any other visible cause. The Mannings soon realized that their house appeared to be the focal point for a paranormal phenomenon known as a poltergeist.

For believers in the paranormal, a poltergeist is an entity that creates a number of different disturbances over a period of time. As psychic researcher and author John Fraser notes, "In medicine a group of symptoms which consistently occur together is called a syndrome and is given a name even if the underlying cause is not known. If a poltergeist was a medical diagnosis it would undoubtedly be a syndrome . . . of strange and often frightening symptoms."[3] Those symptoms would include rapping or knocking sounds on walls, untouched doors opening or closing, cold areas or wet spots appearing without a source, and objects moving by themselves, often flying through the air. In some cases, merely mischievous poltergeists are believed to turn malevolent, igniting fires and physically attacking people. Manifestations of poltergeist activity can last for days, weeks, or, in a few extreme cases, even years.

> "I couldn't believe it when I played the tape back. It sent chills up my spine."[2]
>
> —Lisa Manning, on viewing her poltergeist video

Most people are familiar with haunted houses, where spooky happenings are believed to be signs that a resident ghost haunts those who live or visit there. Poltergeists, however, are believed to attach themselves to a particular person rather than a specific location. In the case of the Manning family, daughter Elle seemed to be the trigger, or "agent," for the poltergeist activity. Studies have shown that young or adolescent girls are more often the choice of agent for poltergeists than are boys. In fact, current paranormal research suggests that girls experiencing the emotional changes of puberty may produce a kind of psychic energy that a poltergeist can use to create its mischief.

Current paranormal research suggests that the emotional changes that girls experience at puberty may produce a kind of psychic energy that a poltergeist can use to create its mischief.

Poltergeists in History

Whether the result of spirits or the psyche, poltergeists have been harassing people for thousands of years. In ancient Egypt, belief in the afterlife was an essential element of society, as the mummified remains of pharaohs interred in imposing, treasure-filled tombs attest. Sometimes an Egyptian's spirit, or *khou*, was said to cross over into the world of the living. Such an event was described in an ancient papyrus that contained a letter written to the spirit of one man's departed wife, Onkhari. A fragment of the papyrus describes the man as being physically assaulted and his home beset by disturbances committed by his late wife's *khou*. "What wrong have I been guilty of," the man beseeches Onkhari, "that I should be in this state of trouble? What have I done that thou should'st help to assail me?"[4] Poltergeist activity was also documented as Western Europe developed. "As early as 858 BC," writes journalist Michael Clarkson, "in a farmhouse in Rhine, Germany . . . an unseen force reportedly threw stones, shook the walls, moved objects, and caused loud banging noises."[5] In particular, the throwing of stones was a common early manifestation of poltergeist activity.

As civilizations developed around the world, reports of poltergeists followed. In 1661 in Tedworth, England, an itinerant street drummer was sued by a man named John Mompesson for extorting money from passersby. The drummer lost the lawsuit, and Mompesson was given the drum. Soon Mompesson's dwelling was inexplicably filled with the relentless sounds of a phantom drummer, both inside the house and on the roof. According to Alfred Owen Aldridge, author and professor of literature, "Mompesson was incessantly disturbed by thumpings and knockings throughout his house. . . . [The drummer] began beating tunes on the children's bedsteads, lifting them out of their beds, and following them around the room."[6] The "Drummer of Tedworth" is often said to be the first example of a poltergeist in England. During the 1730s, a similar noisy spirit was reported in the British colonies in America and was described by Benjamin Franklin in his newspaper, the *Pennsylvania Gazette*.

What Is a Poltergeist?

While researching his 2007 book *The Secret History of Poltergeists and Haunted Houses*, author Claude Lecouteux discovered a mistake in his assumption about peoples' familiarity with poltergeists:

> During the course of my investigation I ran into an unexpected problem. I thought everyone knew what a poltergeist was. Reality taught me otherwise and inspired me to launch an inquiry among my friends, colleagues, and students. I gave the following question to about one hundred people: "What does poltergeist mean to you?" Here are the most significant responses:
>
> "I associate the word poltergeist with an evil spirit. If I remember rightly there was a role-playing game called this about a dozen years ago. I don't remember too much about the game itself, but I know it revolved around ghosts!" J.P., STUDENT
>
> "To me, this word designates a haunted house, in which the haunting manifests not with the appearance of ghosts but by supernatural manifestations. But I could be wrong!" T.M., WRITER
>
> "Poltergeist . . . I am mainly thinking of the film by the same name, but to give a definition, that's hard." S.H., PH.D. STUDENT
>
> "Isn't it a knocking spirit?" J.P.D., BOOKSELLER

Claude Lecouteux, *The Secret History of Poltergeists and Haunted Houses: From Pagan Folklore to Modern Manifestations*. Rochester, VT: Inner Traditions, 2007, pp. 5–6.

Poltergeists and Faith

With all this mysterious activity occurring across many centuries, it is natural that people have tried to understand what lies behind the banging doors and flying furniture. People often turned to their religious faith to seek explanations. The Christian church of Europe during the Middle Ages influenced the belief that unexplained poltergeist activity was linked to the devil or other evil spirits. "Scholars, learned men, and theologians," writes author and professor of medieval civilization Claude Lecouteux, "[observed] that the problem of demons, ghosts, and other unusual manifestations were one of the major concerns of the day."[7]

Victims of poltergeists often asked priests to perform exorcisms to rid their homes of the unsettling disturbances. Martin Luther, who sparked the Protestant Reformation in 1517, often wrote about evil spirits that created poltergeist activity. "It must be acknowledged," Luther wrote, "that people are possessed by the devil, and I have personally experienced wandering spirits who terrify people and prevent them from sleeping, causing them to fall ill."[8] Luther's own poltergeist experiences included loud noises from behind his stove, the sound of clattering plates, and being pelted by hazelnuts from an unseen hand.

> "It must be acknowledged that people are possessed by the devil, and I have personally experienced wandering spirits who terrify people and prevent them from sleeping, causing them to fall ill."[8]
>
> —Protestant reformer Martin Luther

Although religion provided one form of solace against poltergeists, the Age of Enlightenment during the seventeenth and eighteenth centuries presented a new way to view the world: the application of scientific inquiry. Chemistry, physics, biology, and other sciences advanced rational thinking and experimentation to explain many mysteries of the world. Enlightenment scholars used this new way of viewing the world to question the reality of ghosts, demons, and poltergeists. Were they really elements of a spiritual realm, as people had believed for centuries, or could they be explained by logical thought and scientific observation? The answer lay in a new form of faith called Deism—the belief in a supreme being but denying such Christian beliefs as miracles, the devil, demons, and other spiritual traditions that had been a part of the church from its founding. Poltergeists were no longer deemed the evidence of demons or ghosts but were considered natural occurrences that would eventually be explained by science.

From the mid-nineteenth to the early twentieth century there was a rise in public interest in the Spiritualist movement. Spiritualism's central feature was the summoning of poltergeist-like activity to facilitate communication with departed spirits. Self-styled

From the mid-nineteenth to the early twentieth century, self-styled psychic "mediums" promoted their ability to contact spirits in the afterlife through group sessions called séances.

psychic "mediums" promoted their ability to contact spirits in the afterlife through group sessions called séances. Despite skeptics debunking these experiences, many people continued to believe in the supernatural nature of poltergeist activity.

Stages of Poltergeist Activity

Descriptions of poltergeist activity have been relatively consistent through the centuries. A typical poltergeist episode usually goes through several stages, growing more noticeable as the manifestations escalate.

A poltergeist experience usually begins with strange noises, usually a tapping or thumping, that seem to have no source. These are often accompanied by feelings of unease (of being watched by an unknown entity), chills, or anxiety. The next stage can include objects moving on their own, doors or cabinets opening and closing, drawers sliding open and their contents spilled, and items zipping through the air. Some cases include reports of people being levitated, often hovering over their beds as they futilely try to sleep. At this point, it becomes apparent that these weird occurrences are centered around a particular person, known as the agent.

Poltergeists and the Devil

For Martin Luther, poltergeists were the devil's work, as shown in this excerpt from a collection of Luther's dinner-table conversations called *Table Talk,* published in 1566:

> One day when I was weary from reciting my canonical prayers, a loud noise erupted from behind the stove, which terrified me greatly. But when I realized that it was the devil's play I went to bed and prayed to God, saying, "If the Devil has any power over me, let him show it!" And I went to sleep.
>
> Another time, when I was in the refectory, such a loud din of clattering plates erupted, I thought both heaven and earth must be crumbling to pieces, but I soon realized it was the devil at work, at which point I retired and went to sleep. A third time I glanced into the garden from the window of my cell after leaving Mass. I then saw a large black sow racing about in every direction . . . she, too, was the devil. The fourth time occurred when . . . someone was throwing hazelnuts at me from behind the stove. I soon saw this, too, was the work of the devil, so I went to bed.

Quoted in Claude Lecouteux, *The Secret History of Poltergeists and Haunted Houses: From Pagan Folklore to Modern Manifestations.* Rochester, VT: Inner Traditions, 2007, pp. 16–17.

A stage of communication may follow, where the poltergeist interacts with the agent, or even an entire family, by various means, including writing or audible speech. In the Cobb family incident, which centered around an antique bed, the poltergeist was reported to have communicated by writing with crayons on pieces of paper as well as speaking with a disembodied voice. The poltergeist wrote that his name was Jimmy, and his mother had died in the bed. He was angry that anyone else would dare to sleep there and was trying to prevent Jason from doing so.

While most poltergeist incidents are annoying and startling (but generally harmless), a final stage consisting of physical attacks and other violent acts may occur. Victims have been known to complain about being hit, scratched, bitten, or pinched by poltergeists. Other reports include poltergeist activity that destroys property, such as fires that flare up spontaneously without any visible source of ignition.

Poltergeists by the Numbers

The scientific and technological advances of the Age of Enlightenment had a historic impact on the way scholars understood the physical world. But for the common people of the time, the farmers, shopkeepers, and laborers who kept society running, entities such as poltergeists remained a believable explanation for weird happenings. Most people today understand that scientific principles control the universe. Nevertheless, belief in the paranormal is still strong.

In 1979 Alan Gauld and A.D. Cornell, two British experts in parapsychology (the study of psychic phenomena) conducted a computerized statistical analysis of poltergeist activity dating back to the early nineteenth century. With a goal of uncovering five hundred cases of strange incidents that could be connected to poltergeists, the researchers soon struggled to limit their survey to just five hundred examples. Apparently, poltergeists had been even more active throughout history than they had realized. The survey was an exhaustive compilation of activities that were attributed to poltergeists, and it showed how frequently they appeared in reports spanning several centuries.

The study revealed that more than half the cases occurred at night, and the poltergeist activity most-often reported was the moving of small objects. Nearly one-third of the cases involved a female agent under twenty years old. Rapping or knocking noises, the trademark of poltergeist encounters, occurred in almost half of the cases, followed by voices, groans, and other humanlike sounds.

In all, sixty-three separate categories of activities related to poltergeists were evaluated, from bedclothes being disturbed and foul odors permeating a house to objects passing through walls and animals showing signs of stress. In their book *Poltergeists*, Gauld and Cornell concluded,

> The chief point of emphasis that seems to emerge is that it is not just "simple" poltergeist phenomena, like raps and object movements, that have been more frequently reported in the better-evidenced cases, but the more complex and bizarre phenomena too—for instance, objects appearing in mid-air, apparitions of all kinds . . . possession or obsession [and] levitation of the human body.[9]

Phenomena such as bodies appearing in mid-air are among the more bizarre examples of poltergeist activity.

Statistical studies, as valuable as they can be, go only so far when considering paranormal subjects. The numbers tell us how many times a certain poltergeist activity was reported, where it happened, and who observed it. What statistics cannot show is how people are affected by these incidents. This is where the stories that people tell about their experiences come in: whether they were frightened or merely curious; how they reacted to an unknown situation; and what their education, religious beliefs, and psychological makeup tell them about the source of the incident. These are the stories that make the subject of poltergeists fascinating and often challenging to understand.

> "It is not just 'simple' poltergeist phenomena, like raps and object movements, that have been more frequently reported in the better-evidenced cases, but the more complex and bizarre phenomena too—for instance, objects appearing in mid-air, apparitions of all kinds . . . possession or obsession [and] levitation of the human body."[9]
>
> —Parapsychologists Alan Gauld and A.D. Cornell

Mischievous Poltergeists

Tourism has been a staple of Florida's economy since the early 1920s, and souvenirs have always been a part of the vacation experience. Travelers from other states and foreign countries enjoy purchasing mementos as a reminder of their visit to the Sunshine State. Tropication Arts was a wholesaler of souvenir items, storing thousands of Florida-themed merchandise in its Miami warehouse. In late 1966, Tropication employees reported that products were flying off the shelves—literally—as a poltergeist appeared to have invaded the company's stockroom.

During that year's winter tourist season, Tropication Arts was busy fulfilling orders for souvenir mugs, glasses, ceramic collectibles, and hundreds of other novelties. In December, co-owner Alvin Laubheim began noticing an increase in breakage among his stock. After several weeks of falling items, Laubheim began to suspect two shipping clerks, Curt Hagemeyer and Julio Vasquez. Believing they had become careless in their work habits, he instructed them in proper storage techniques. "From then on," Laubheim later related, "everything started to happen—boxes came down—a box of about a hundred back-scratchers turned over and fell with a terrific clatter over on the other side of the room and then we realized that there was something definitely wrong around here."[10]

Other employees also observed boxes and glass items falling from shelves without being pushed or otherwise touched. Debris constantly had to be swept up, with broken glass making it particularly hazardous to work in the warehouse. As the damage continued to mount in January 1967, Laubheim decided that it was time to seek help.

Bringing in the Experts

A number of people became involved in the investigation of the mysterious poltergeist activity at Tropication. First to arrive at the warehouse was Miami police officer William Killin. As he walked among the shelves, he saw a glass fall unassisted to the floor and noticed some other items that had also tumbled from their places. Killin called for backup, bringing two more patrolmen and a sergeant to the scene. The newly arrived officers also witnessed items falling from the storage shelves. Over the next several days, witnesses included Susy Smith, a parapsychologist; Sinclair Buntin, a friend of Smith; and Howard Brooks, a magician. They all tried to figure out what was happening, looking for such possible causes as mild earth tremors, the building's foundation shifting, vibrations from passing trucks, and even sonic booms caused by jet airplanes. As a professional magician, Brooks searched for signs of trickery but found none.

When boxes of merchandise such as coffee mugs and drinking glasses mysteriously began falling from shelves at the souvenir wholesaler Tropication Arts in Miami, the firm's owner called for help from two noted parapsychologists, William G. Roll and Gaither Pratt.

To conduct a methodical examination of the Tropication poltergeist, two noted parapsychologists, William G. Roll and Gaither Pratt, were called in. Employees told them that nineteen-year-old shipping clerk Vasquez always seemed to be present when breakage occurred, leading them to believe that he was causing the trouble. After conducting a series of controlled experiments and observing Vasquez, the investigators concluded that the young clerk was not causing the damage by trickery. But Roll sensed that Vasquez might still be the source of the poltergeist activity.

Vasquez's Mind

According to Roll, Vasquez, a Cuban refugee, seemed to lead a troubled life, harboring feelings of guilt and anger that he struggled to suppress. Roll suggested that these troubling emotions could be relieved by physical phenomena that appear without Vasquez's awareness. Roll had studied such phenomena and theorized that certain people could move objects using only their mind, without conscious knowledge or control.

When Vasquez was asked how he felt about the breakage, he replied, "I feel happy: that thing [the breakage] makes me feel happy. I don't know why."[11] He later stated that he felt nervous when the unusual poltergeist activity did not occur for a period of time. Roll and Pratt went on to write several papers on the subject. When Vasquez was later fired from Tropication, the strange events ceased. With other explanations discarded, it appeared that the Miami poltergeist could have been bizarre activity in the mind of a nineteen-year-old shipping clerk, not a supernatural entity.

The Rosenheim Poltergeist

Another workplace poltergeist event occurred nearly a year after the Tropication incident in an office halfway around the world in the southern German town of Rosenheim. Although separated by time and distance, the two events shared an eerie similarity: a nineteen-year-old employee who appeared to be the poltergeist's agent.

The Toy Store Poltergeist

Probably the last place to find paranormal activity would be a store filled with colorful toys and cute stuffed animals—and located in a place called Sunnyvale. Yet during the 1970s a poltergeist named Jan brought chaos to a toy store in the quiet California town.

The Toys "R" Us store in Sunnyvale was built in 1970, and for years enthralled wide-eyed children with aisles of dolls, games, and Lego sets. But employees began experiencing strange things in 1978, as toys launched themselves off the shelves, workers felt eerie sensations of being watched, and restroom faucets turned themselves on and off. A psychic was called in and told of a tragedy that happened during the 1800s on a farm at the store's location. A farmhand named Jan Johnson, spurned by the woman he loved, accidentally died during a fit of grief and rage. It seemed that he had returned to vent his psychic anger.

The Toys "R" Us eventually closed, and the building sat vacant for years until reborn in 2021 as a camping outfitters store. As for Johnson, he had apparently moved on because the spooky activity never reappeared.

In the fall of 1967, lawyer Sigmund Adam hired a new employee for his law firm: a nineteen-year-old secretary named Annemarie Schaberl. Soon after she settled into her job, strange things started occurring. First, the office's telephone system began malfunctioning, abruptly disconnecting in the middle of a call and constantly ringing with no one on the other end. The firm started to receive steep bills for an enormous number of calls—so many that it was physically impossible for the employees to have made them.

Next, the office's electrical system went haywire. Light fixtures began swinging for no apparent reason. Incandescent bulbs and fluorescent tubes randomly flickered on and off and sometimes became loose in their sockets. Several electrical power surges caused the office's lights to explode. Other weird phenomena reported included desk drawers opening and closing, pictures spinning and falling from their places on the walls, and a copy machine leaking chemicals. In one astonishing incident, employees said a 400-pound (181.4 kg) filing cabinet moved by itself, scratching the floor as it went.

The Investigation Begins

Adam called on experts in different specialties to try to figure out what was going on. Engineers from the company that installed the office machines and telephones could find nothing wrong with the office equipment. The malfunctions continued even after the old equipment was replaced. Technicians checked the telephone lines, but no problems were found. Electricians examined the electrical service going into the building and installed a meter to determine the cause of the power surges. Even after isolating the law office from the town's main power station and using electricity from a generator, the surges continued. After exhausting all possible physical causes for the disturbances, a frustrated Adam turned to an expert in the paranormal.

Hans Bender, a professor of parapsychology at the University of Freiburg in Germany, was an expert in the fringe areas of psychology, including ESP and poltergeists. "I've investigated 38 poltergeist cases," Bender said in a 1974 interview with a Pittsburgh newspaper reporter, "and believe me, they defy normal scientific

A lawyer's office in the southern German town of Rosenheim (shown) was the site of a workplace poltergeist event.

explanation."[12] Bender arrived at Adam's office in December 1967 and immediately went to work studying the details of the case. He set up a video camera to record any new activity from the suspected poltergeist and was rewarded by capturing footage of light fixtures swinging. In his investigation, Bender noted that no poltergeist activity occurred on weekends when the office was closed, leading him to believe an employee somehow triggered the events by trickery or other means. Bender soon narrowed his suspicions down to one person: Annemarie Schaberl.

> "I've investigated 38 poltergeist cases and believe me, they defy normal scientific explanation."[12]
>
> —Professor of parapsychology Hans Bender

A Disturbed Mind

In conversations with Schaberl, Bender discovered that she was bored at her job and troubled by a contentious relationship with her strict father. Bender brought her to his laboratory to test her for signs of paranormal abilities. Although the results were negative, after further examination Bender became convinced that Schaberl's repressed anger at her life situation was causing the chaos at the law office. He believed that the strange events involved psychokinesis (PK), the supposed ability to move objects using only one's mind. "These disturbances come from actual emotional disorder," Bender noted. "These people are usually young, often adolescents, with very intense conflicts. . . . The emotional conflict is converted into PK which causes the phenomena."[13]

When Schaberl left her job in January 1968, things returned to normal at Sigmund Adam's law office. For Bender, the Rosenheim case was a milestone in paranormal investigations: It was the first time a video recording captured purported evidence of a poltergeist in action.

A Poltergeist in Enfield

When poltergeists disrupt businesses, firms like Tropication and Sigmund Adam's law practice can lose money, customers, and sometimes even their reputations. But when the focus of poltergeist

Paranormal Research Groups

As interest in the paranormal gained momentum during the late nineteenth century, groups of researchers formed societies to consolidate their resources and promote scientific methods for psychic investigations. The oldest of these organizations is the Society for Psychical Research (SPR). Established in London in 1882, the SPR dedicated itself to exploring the realm of the unknown by investigating ghosts, hauntings, ESP, Spiritualism, and poltergeist activity. The SPR conducted investigations in numerous high-profile cases, including the Enfield poltergeist.

In America, the Ghost Research Society was founded in 1977 in the Chicago area as a clearinghouse for reports of ghosts, poltergeists, and other paranormal phenomena. With regional coordinators in several states, the organization conducts research into paranormal activity and analyzes such evidence as spirit photographs, audio recordings, and videos.

On the skeptical side of the poltergeist phenomenon is the international Committee for Skeptical Inquiry (CSI), dedicated to promoting the use of reason in paranormal investigation. Joe Nickell is the CSI's senior research fellow and its leading investigator. He believes paranormal mysteries should "neither be hyped nor dismissed, but instead carefully investigated with a view toward solving them." Nickell is believed to be the world's only full-time paranormal investigator.

Quoted in Bob Rickard, "The Levitations of St Joseph of Copertino: Explained?," *Journal for the Study of Religious Experience*, Vol. 9, No. 1 (2023), p. 71.

---

activity is ordinary individuals in their homes, the stakes are much higher. The stress of dealing with inexplicable phenomena can ruin a family's tranquil life.

Since 1964 the Hodgson family had lived peacefully in a modest house at 284 Green Street in Enfield, a quiet borough of North London. But in the summer of 1977, Peggy Hodgson and her four children—Janet, Margaret, Johnny, and Billy—began a paranormal journey that lasted nearly two years. On August 30, 1977, Janet and Johnny, who shared a bedroom, felt their beds shaking and heard rapping noises on the walls. The next night the disturbances grew worse, with a large chest of drawers moving by itself, seemingly attempting to block the room's doorway. Peggy tried unsuccessfully to return the chest to its place. "I just couldn't believe it," she later recalled. "In fact I pushed it back twice, and a third time I couldn't move it."[14] A panicking Peggy gathered up her children and fled to the safety of her next-door neighbors' house.

The neighbors, Vic Nottingham and his son, Gary, searched the Hodgson house but did not encounter moving furniture, although they reported hearing some knocking sounds. Nottingham called the police, and two officers soon arrived. Constable Carolyn Heeps witnessed a kitchen chair slide across the floor and heard more knocking sounds, but with no sign of an actual crime, there was little the officers could do.

Witnessing Poltergeist Activity

With the police promising to keep an eye on their house, the Hodgsons returned to their home and sought help from the media. The *Daily Mirror* newspaper sent a reporter and photographer to see whether there was a story worth pursuing. They did not have to wait long for an answer because "suddenly all these things started flying around the room," said photographer Graham Morris. "It was really unnerving. I got struck above my eyebrow with a Lego brick with some force. The kids were just in such a state, screaming and crying."[15] Morris spent numerous hours in the house over a period of eighteen months. He set up cameras with remote or time-lapse triggers so he could take pictures when he was not in a room when poltergeist activity occurred. Several of his photographs capture frightening images of Janet appearing to levitate above her bed. The story of the Enfield poltergeist made the front page of the *Daily Mirror* on September 10, 1977.

> "Suddenly all these things started flying around the room. It was really unnerving. I got struck above my eyebrow with a Lego brick with some force. The kids were just in such a state, screaming and crying."[15]
>
> —Photographer Graham Morris

Although Morris's photographs show what happened, they do not reveal why such things occurred. Two parapsychologists were called in to try to discover the force behind the poltergeist activity. Maurice Grosse arrived on September 8 and was soon joined by Guy Lyon Playfair. For several months the two investigators documented hundreds of unusual events, including rapping and banging, furniture moving, and curtains and bedclothes becoming unaccountably twisted. But the most bizarre episodes were when Janet began speaking in the gruff and raspy voice of what was presumed to be an old man. What started as growls and barks from Janet became a voice that Grosse conversed with. Often sounding angry and using profanity, quite the opposite of Janet's usual way of speaking, the voice said his name was

In the summer of 1977, parapsychologist Maurice Grosse (pictured) was called in to investigate poltergeist activity at a home in the North London borough of Enfield.

Joe (he later changed it to Bill) who had once lived—and died—in the Green Street house. Grosse recorded hours of his conversations with the voice through Janet, during which she seemed to be in a trance.

Real or Hoax?

With Janet appearing to be the poltergeist's agent, she was subjected to both physical and psychiatric examinations by doctors and therapists. A study of her vocal cords using an electronic device that produced images of sound waves made by the human larynx revealed that the voice of Joe/Bill was totally different than her own natural voice. She could not have been faking the voice without damaging her vocal cords. Then, in a surprising turn of events, Janet's older sister, Margaret, also began to speak in an old man's voice. This coincidence caused some investigators to wonder whether the Enfield poltergeist was nothing more than a prank played by two mischievous girls enjoying the attention they received.

> "I'm 100 percent, no 150 percent, satisfied that this case was genuine poltergeist activity."[17]
>
> —Paranormal researcher Maurice Grosse

In 1987 Margaret wrote a letter declaring, "Everything that happened in the . . . case was perfectly true. Nothing was faked."[16] But the accusation of the use of some trickery by the girls could not be overlooked. Janet admitted that she and her sister had indeed played some tricks because they became bored when the poltergeist activity occasionally tapered off. But she estimated that only about 2 percent of the disturbances were caused by their pranks.

For Grosse, the evidence of poltergeist activity was impossible to ignore. Photographs, video and sound recordings, and the personal observation of more than fifteen hundred strange events by more than thirty witnesses, including police officers and scientists, all combined to create what has been called the most-investigated poltergeist case of all time. Despite the girls' admission of trickery, Grosse said in a 2005 interview, "I'm 100 percent, no 150 percent, satisfied that this case was genuine poltergeist activity."[17]

Dangerous Poltergeists

Poltergeists are sometimes characterized as mischievous pranksters who delight in playing tricks on unsuspecting victims. Rapping on walls, moving furniture, and making objects fly across a room can be unnerving but are usually harmless antics. Not all poltergeist activity is benign, however. Poltergeists have been reported to subject people to physical harm or psychological trauma as well as to cause damage to property. This destruction includes fires of unexplained origin. In 1941, one family was plagued by dozens of mysterious blazes that broke out in a single day at their farmhouse.

A Poltergeist Fire Starter

Fifty-nine-year-old William Hackler owned a small farm near the town of Odon in southern Indiana. To supplement his farm income, Hackler also worked as a deliveryman for a local dairy company. On Friday, June 21, 1941, Hackler was on his morning route when he received word of a fire at his house. Learning that the fire was not serious, Hackler decided to complete his deliveries and then headed for home. Upon his arrival, Hackler's wife, Minnie, told him that a small fire had started in an upstairs bedroom of the two-story dwelling. Firefighters, arriving in the small town's only fire truck, had quickly extinguished the flames but were puzzled about the fire's origin. Believing that the wall might be hiding an old, defective chimney, the men broke through the plaster wall but found nothing behind it: oddly, the fire had only burned the wallpaper on the surface.

Soon after the fire truck left the Hackler home, another fire broke out, this time burning the wallpaper of another bedroom. Returning to the scene, the firefighters once more doused the flames. Yet again they were at a loss to explain the source of the fire. The Hacklers hoped that the strange fires were somehow just freak occurrences, but their nightmare was just beginning.

Twenty-Eight Blazes

Throughout the day, more mysterious fires cropped up in a strangely random manner. A blaze began in a pair of Hackler's overalls that had been hanging behind a door. Flames arose in a downstairs bed and inside a book. A calendar hanging on a wall caught fire. From 8:00 to 11:00 that morning, nine separate fires broke out, with the Hackler family putting them out as they occurred. Flames continued to erupt throughout the day amid fears that the entire house might become engulfed. As neighbors flocked to the house to help the Hacklers, they observed the bizarre events. "It was like unseen hands were lighting matches all over the house,"[18] one witness commented. By the end of the day, a total of twenty-eight fires had been extinguished, leaving the Hacklers shaken and exhausted.

A Spooky Past

Although the family had lived in the farmhouse for a decade, the place had a tragic history prior to their arrival. The original owners had died during the 1880s from typhoid, which back then was often referred to as "the burning fever." The son of a later occupant was killed in a hunting accident and buried on the property. The grieving father said that his son communicated via knocking sounds in the house, the hallmark of poltergeist activity. Many witnesses believed the house was cursed, claiming that this was

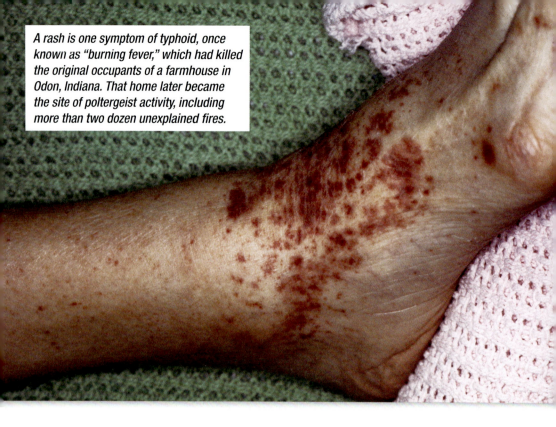

A rash is one symptom of typhoid, once known as "burning fever," which had killed the original occupants of a farmhouse in Odon, Indiana. That home later became the site of poltergeist activity, including more than two dozen unexplained fires.

proof of a supernatural source of the fires. Other explanations were also considered: lightning heating up nails in the woodwork, spontaneous combustion, a volatile chemical self-igniting, and even faulty electrical wiring (the latter was easily debunked because the house had no electricity).

Weary from their unsettling experience, the Hackler family dismantled the house and rebuilt it in a nearby location. If a poltergeist was indeed the incendiary culprit, it apparently stayed behind, for the Hacklers were no longer troubled by mysterious fires. No reasonable explanation has ever been found for the poltergeist fires of Odon.

Burning in Macomb

Some 300 miles (483 km) separate Odon from the town of Macomb in western Illinois. In 1948 a Macomb family experienced frightening fires similar to those that plagued the Hackler family. Although eight years separated the incidents, the terror of mysterious fires had the same effect on both families.

In 1948 the family of Arthur McNeil was torn apart by a bitter divorce. McNeil, who had custody of his two children, eight-year-old Arthur Jr. and thirteen-year-old Wanet, moved his family to live with relatives Charles and Lou Willey on their farm near Macomb. The Willeys had offered to help raise the children. Little did they realize the misfortune that was about to befall them.

The trouble first appeared as a brown spot on a wall of the Willey house. More spots soon developed and began smoldering, ultimately bursting into flames. McNeil and the Willeys were soon dashing from fire to fire, dousing the flames with water buckets placed strategically around the house. Neighbors came to help, some sleeping on the floor to be ready for quick response to the fiery outbreaks. Macomb's fire chief, Fred Wilson, and the deputy state fire marshal, John Burgard, arrived to investigate but could discover no explanation for the strange blazes. "Nobody ever heard anything like it," said Burgard, "but I saw it with my own eyes. . . . Everybody thought there were ghosts around there."[19] And still the fires continued, breaking out on the front porch and on the house's ceilings, and burning curtains and other objects.

> "Nobody ever heard anything like it, but I saw it with my own eyes. . . . Everybody thought there were ghosts around there."[19]
>
> —Illinois fire marshal John Burgard

Up in Flames

Over the next week some two hundred unexplained fires broke out throughout the Willey house. Then, on August 14, flames consumed the entire five-room dwelling, burning it to its foundation. The following days saw fires damage a milk storage building and two barns, leaving the Willey farm a scene of desolation with only a few small outbuildings left standing.

Despite the rural locale and small population of Macomb, national newspapers soon picked up the story. Public interest in the mysterious fires grew, and on August 22 more than one thousand curious people swarmed the Willey farm, gawking at the ruined buildings while advancing theories about the source of the fires.

The Jaboticabal Poltergeist

Jaboticabal is a municipality in southeastern Brazil, about 190 miles (306 km) from Brazil's largest city, São Paulo. The story of the Jaboticabal poltergeist is one of most vicious and tragic encounters with poltergeist activity in the annals of paranormal research. And it centers around an innocent young girl.

During the mid-1960s, Maria José Ferreira was happily living with her family in Jaboticabal. But things changed for the eleven-year-old in December 1965 when strange events began to occur. Bricks, some weighing up to 8 pounds (3.6 kg), were said to have flown around the house, hitting Maria and damaging furniture. The girl suffered other injuries believed to have been caused by the unseen entity, including being bitten, slapped, pelted with stones, and pierced with needles. At one point, more than fifty needles had to be removed from her foot. On several occasions, Maria's clothing mysteriously caught fire.

Being devout Catholics, the family arranged for an exorcism, but the attacks on Maria got worse, continuing for several years. Ultimately the poltergeist activity abated somewhat, but it was too late. In 1970 Maria was found dead in her room, a victim of suicide.

Investigators from the Willey family's insurance company, the National Underwriters Fire Laboratories, showed up. So did representatives of the US Air Force, who confirmed that no foreign interference was involved. The air force and insurance investigators studied the evidence. Causes proposed included radio waves, flammable wallpaper paste, faulty electrical wiring, and combustible gases within the walls of the house. Although each theory was dismissed, a solution presented itself on August 30.

Teenage Fire Starter

Stumped for an explanation for the mysterious fires, Marshal Burgard decided to interview the family members, starting with Wanet. After an hour-long interrogation, Wanet finally admitted to starting the fires using ordinary kitchen matches. When pressed for details about the fires, she said, "What ones? I set them all."[20] Devastated by her parents' divorce, Wanet believed that by destroying the Willey farm she would be sent to live with her mother in Bloomington, Illinois, about 100 miles (161 km) away. "She's a nice little kid caught in the middle of a broken home,"[21] explained

Dr. Sophie Schroeder, a psychiatrist who examined Wanet. Newspapers printed the confession, and interest in the strange fires in Macomb soon died out.

But questions arose that sowed seeds of doubt about Wanet's story. Could she really have set more than two hundred fires (including raging blazes that destroyed three buildings) just using matches she found in the house? It also seemed unlikely that with so many witnesses milling around the Willey home, no one observed her setting any of the fires. Some skeptics believed that Burgard had coerced Wanet to confess in order to protect his reputation and bring a tidy resolution to a baffling case.

Then again, Wanet certainly fit the profile of a poltergeist's agent, a teenage girl going through a difficult time of life. Perhaps she had unwittingly caused the fires through the power of her troubled mind and made up the story of the matches. Despite the well-publicized resolution of the case, one paranormal researcher called it a perfect example of poltergeist phenomena.

Poltergeists Who Terrorize

Fires that appear out of nowhere are obviously upsetting to the people they impact. But fire is not the only way that poltergeists are believed to harass their victims. Poltergeist activity can become even more personal, more frightening, and more dangerous. A poltergeist encounter of this sort took place in the early 2000s in the town of South Shields, located in northeast England.

Marianne Peterworth and her three-year-old son, Robert, shared a modest house in South Shields with her boyfriend, Marc Karlsonn. (All of the names have been changed for privacy.) Their household was peaceful until late 2005, when strange happenings—later described as typical poltergeist activity—turned their world upside down. For no apparent reason, tables and chairs were found out of place, Robert's stuffed animals and other toys flew across his bedroom, and blankets were pulled off beds by invisible hands. By the next summer

One sign of poltergeist activity is a pet that shows signs of distress for no apparent reason.

the bizarre activity had gotten worse, and so had the couple's panic. Even their pet dog and cat became distressed, growling and hissing at an unseen entity. Paranormal researcher Darren Ritson, who helped investigate the case, noted that "incidents such as this make it almost irresistible to conclude that the primary focus of this entity is to instill fear, dread and terror into its victims."[22] Ritson was convinced that the chilling events in South Shields were real poltergeist activity, a case he says he will never forget.

> "Incidents such as this make it almost irresistible to conclude that the primary focus of this entity is to instill fear, dread and terror into its victims."[22]
>
> —Paranormal researcher Darren Ritson

Poltergeist Attacks

Along with moving tables and flying toys, the South Shields poltergeist soon began a series of personal attacks. "Marianne," Karlsonn said, "there's something else wrong. My body feels like it's burning."[23] He removed his T-shirt to reveal thirteen scratches on his torso. Later that day, more scratches and bloody cuts appeared on Karlsonn's body, and he complained of feeling hot and generally unwell. Along with Karlsonn's physical injuries, Peterworth was plagued with threatening texts on her cellphone. One message ominously read, "Going to die today, going to get you." Then another, "I can get you when you awake and I'll come for you when you're asleep."[24] Oddly, the texts appeared to be coming from Karlsonn's phone even though he had disabled it by removing its battery.

More troubling signs appeared. A kitchen knife was found on a table in Robert's bedroom, arranged on two stuffed animals to appear as though one were slashing the other; other knives reportedly flew around the kitchen, some barely missing Peterworth. Karlsonn said he was repeatedly pelted with flying objects, including items from Robert's toy workbench. The suspected poltergeist continued to torment the family for about a

Hollywood Poltergeists

When the story of a poltergeist turning malevolent and wreaking physical harm on innocent people begins to circulate, it is likely that the movie industry will turn it into a big-screen fright fest. Several popular movies have been based on the evil actions of a malicious poltergeist. One of the most popular films of this genre was the blockbuster *Poltergeist*, released in theaters across America in 1982. The film's family becomes terrorized by a poltergeist that invades their quiet suburban home through their television set. The family's five-year-old daughter, Carol Anne, communicates with the entity, which soon drags her into another dimension.

While a fictional story, *Poltergeist* was inspired by the 1958 Seaford poltergeist, where bottles and other objects were said to be manipulated by unseen forces. It became one of the most publicized poltergeist cases of the twentieth century.

Another film, 2016's *The Conjuring 2*, was based on the Enfield poltergeist case that took place in England in 1977. The movie's plot revolves around the poltergeist activity that disrupted the Hodgson family, especially their daughter Janet. As befitting a Hollywood drama, the villainous poltergeist is vanquished in the end. Although the real-life Janet later admitted to some trickery, the actual cause of the Enfield poltergeist remains unclear.

year; after a respite, it returned for one more week of terror before finally departing for good.

A notable difference between this case and a typical poltergeist event is the lack of a young girl acting as the poltergeist's agent. Karlsonn, however, had suffered the tragic loss of a family member shortly before the mysterious events began, although he outwardly showed little sorrow. Perhaps in suppressing his grief his mind became the trigger that brought violent activity to the quiet home in South Shields.

The Pontefract Poltergeist

From South Shields to the town of Pontefract is a distance of about 100 miles (161 km). Pontefract has gained a dubious reputation due to a seemingly ordinary red brick house located at 30 East Drive. As British television personality Yvette Fielding found out, the house is anything but ordinary. "I have never been so frightened in my life,"[25] Fielding says of the time she and her crew spent investigating the strange occurrences at the house. Fielding is host of the British paranormal reality show *Most Haunted Live*, which aired its investigation of the house on October 31, 2015. According to an account in the *Yorkshire Evening Post*, "Fielding claims that during

The seemingly ordinary red brick house at 30 East Drive in the English town of Pontefract became the site of extremely violent poltergeist activity.

filming, a crucifix was thrown at members of the crew, they saw a carving knife stand upright, two crew members were burned, one passed out and a demonic voice was recorded."[26]

The Poltergeist Returns

The story of the Pontefract poltergeist actually begins nearly fifty years before the *Most Haunted Live* broadcast. In 1966 Joe and Jean Pritchard and their children, Phillip and Diane, were living in the house on East Drive when strange things began to happen. Cold spots could be felt in the house, and unexplained puddles of water appeared in various rooms. After these initial incidents, two years passed before the poltergeist-like activity returned, this time becoming more violent. Loud noises disturbed the family, and objects were reported to move by themselves, often flying through the house and barely missing the occupants. A grandfather clock was destroyed after it tumbled down the stairs with no one nearby who could have caused its fall.

> "[Pontefract] has an amazing reputation of having the most violent poltergeist in Europe or the world and I can categorically confirm that is the case."[27]
>
> —Reality show host Yvette Fielding

The Pritchards' daughter, Diane, was twelve years old, around the typical age for a girl to become a poltergeist agent. And she seemed to become the focus of the weird events. On several occasions she was violently thrown from her bed, and once she was purportedly dragged up the stairs by an unseen force, causing red marks to appear on her throat as if made by an invisible hand. In another incident, the family said the poltergeist attempted to strangle Diane with an electrical cord.

The Pontefract poltergeist has been memorialized in several books, a feature film, and even has its own website. Tours and overnight stays in the famous house are available, and many tourists have reported witnessing unexplainable goings-on. For Fielding, Pontefract lingers as a spooky place in her memory. "It has an amazing reputation of having the most violent poltergeist in Europe or the world and I can categorically confirm that is the case."[27]

CHAPTER FOUR

Seeking the Truth

It started as a seemingly typical poltergeist event. In April 1974, two girls in the town of Andover, England, began hearing rapping noises coming from the wall of the bedroom they shared. Rather than being frightened by the mysterious sounds, the girls, Theresa and Maria Andrews, were intrigued. They decided to see whether they could communicate with the unknown entity rapping on their wall.

Devising a code where one knock from the entity meant *yes* and two meant *no*, the girls began to ask simple yes-or-no questions. These sessions soon evolved into more complicated communication, using raps that stood for letters of the alphabet: one for *a*, two for *b*, and so on. Soon the entire Andrews family had joined in communicating with the poltergeist. They learned, among other things, that the entity's name was Eric. The ritual of asking questions and receiving knocks as answers continued until near the middle of June, when Eric stopped responding. With that, the Andover poltergeist was gone for good.

At the time of the incidents one of the girls, Theresa, was twelve years old, leading investigators to suggest her as the poltergeist agent. Although no psychological tests were performed on her, investigators believed that it could have been her subconscious mind generating the rapping noises.

Some thought the Andrews family had found something that humans for centuries had longed for: the ability to contact those who have crossed the boundary between the physical world and a realm that lies beyond. During the nineteenth century, many people believed the activities caused by poltergeists seemed to show that something did indeed exist beyond this life. And there were many others who willingly encouraged belief in that existence.

Spiritualist Sisters

More than one hundred years before the two Andrews girls began communicating with the poltergeist at their Andover home, two other sisters were attempting the same feat in the small town of Hydesville in upstate New York. The farmhouse in which they lived had been the scene of poltergeist activity that troubled the previous owners of the house with rapping sounds on the walls and furniture. When John and Margaret Fox's family, which included their two young daughters, Maggie and Kate, moved into the house, they also heard the nightly rapping on the walls. This gave eleven-year-old Kate an idea.

Kate and Maggie Fox, along with their older sister, Leah (center), popularized the idea that the spirits of dead people could communicate with the living.

> "The ghost not only answers all questions put to it, but readily gives the age of each child in the family, and of others in the neighborhood."[28]
>
> —New York's *Rochester Daily Advertiser* newspaper

She began questioning the noisy entity and received answers using the same kind of code the Andrews sisters would later employ: one tap for *yes* and two taps for *no*. "The excitement in reference to the mysterious knocking in a house at Hydesville . . . still continues," read an article in the May 7, 1848, edition of New York's *Rochester Daily Advertiser*. "The ghost not only answers all questions put to it, but readily gives the age of each child in the family, and of others in the neighborhood."[28] Word of the girls' amazing ability quickly spread, and soon they were demonstrating their spirit-communication skills to growing crowds of local residents. Later, Kate and Maggie moved to Rochester, New York, to live with their older sister, Leah. Leah managed the girls' public appearances, which had grown so popular that paying crowds filled the stately Corinthian Hall, Rochester's newest and grandest auditorium. Not only was the public enthralled, but a new religion called Spiritualism also emerged from the Fox sisters' demonstrations.

Signs from the Spirit World

While Spiritualism shared with other, more traditional religions the belief that the human spirit lives beyond death, it also promoted the idea that these departed spirits can communicate with the living. The demonstrations of the Fox sisters seemed to prove that such communication was possible, and in just a few years their popularity swept the nation.

Séances, or gatherings of people hoping to speak to the departed, became popular in the United States and soon all over the world. Although the term *poltergeist* was not used in relation to these séances, some very poltergeist-like activity was the centerpiece of the meetings. Tables and other furniture would rock, tip, or levitate, items would appear and disappear without any observable cause, and participants often felt the sensation of being touched by spirit hands. Communicating with the spirits was accomplished by various means, including messages written on small chalkboards called spirit slates, music played on instruments that seemed to float in midair, knocking and rapping noises, and speaking directly to the spirits and hearing their answers.

Despite its popularity, skeptics viewed Spiritualism as a scam that targeted gullible individuals. The skeptics were vindicated when, forty years after the Fox sisters first encountered the rapping spirit, Maggie confessed that she and Kate had been "perpetrating the fraud of Spiritualism upon a too confiding public."[29] She revealed how she and Kate had created the rapping noises by manipulating the joints in their fingers and toes. A change of heart prompted Maggie to retract her confession in 1889, but it was too late to halt the eventual decline of Spiritualism. It still had its believers, however, and the 1920s saw a resurgence of interest in Spiritualism.

Houdini's Ultimate Challenge

Despite magician Harry Houdini's crusade to expose the fraudulent nature of Spiritualism, on a deeper, personal level he embraced the possibility of communicating with the dead. He made a pact with his wife, Bess, that, should he die before her, he would try to contact her from beyond with a coded message only they knew.

On October 22, 1926, Houdini allowed a fan to deliver several punches to his abdomen as a test of the magician's strength. In great pain, Houdini nevertheless performed that night, unaware that his appendix had been ruptured by the blows, mortally injuring him. Nine days later, on Halloween, the great Houdini passed away.

Bess vowed to carry out their plan, and the next year she held a séance on October 31 in hopes of receiving Houdini's message. Although disappointed when the message did not come through, she remained optimistic. For ten years, Bess held a séance every Halloween but never heard from her departed husband. At the final séance in 1936, she lamented, "My last hope is gone. . . . I now, reverently, turn out the light. It is finished. Good night, Harry!"

Quoted in Neely Tucker, "Hollywood, Houdini and the Halloween Seance of 1936," *Timeless* (blog), Library of Congress, October 30, 2020. https://blogs.loc.gov.

Revival in the Twenties

The roaring twenties was a decade of good times: World War I was over, jazz became a popular style of music, and risqué dancing filled crowded nightclubs. Spiritualism was once again widespread, perhaps as an antidote for the excesses of the era. As in the late nineteenth century, poltergeist activity once more became cloaked in the guise of a religious revival. As séances with rapping and furniture moving again grew in popularity, skeptics once more searched for the truth behind these phenomena. Two famous men, one a believer and the other a skeptic, embodied the division between belief in the supernatural and distrust in what is presented as fact.

A Strange Friendship

Arthur Conan Doyle is most famous as the creator of Sherlock Holmes, the fictional detective who used deductive reasoning to solve crimes. Over forty years, beginning in 1886, Doyle penned more than fifty stories and four novels featuring Holmes. In an ironic twist of fate, the author of the logical detective was a staunch believer in Spiritualism, claiming that he had communicated with the spirits of both his departed son and his mother.

During the 1920s, Doyle became friends with magician Harry Houdini, famous for his incredible feats of escape from handcuffs, chains, and water-filled tanks. Impressed by the magician, Doyle even suggested that Houdini was employing supernatural means in his escapes, a claim that the magician vehemently denied. Houdini used his knowledge of magic techniques to discredit Spiritualist frauds. He demonstrated that the moving of tables, rapping noises, and disembodied voices during séances were produced by simple trickery and misdirection.

Both men wrote books championing their respective opinions of Spiritualism. Houdini's *A Magician Among the Spirits* describes how he exposed the tricks of spirit mediums, and Doyle's *The History of Spiritualism* is a two-volume work on the history and doctrines of Spiritualism. Their personal differences

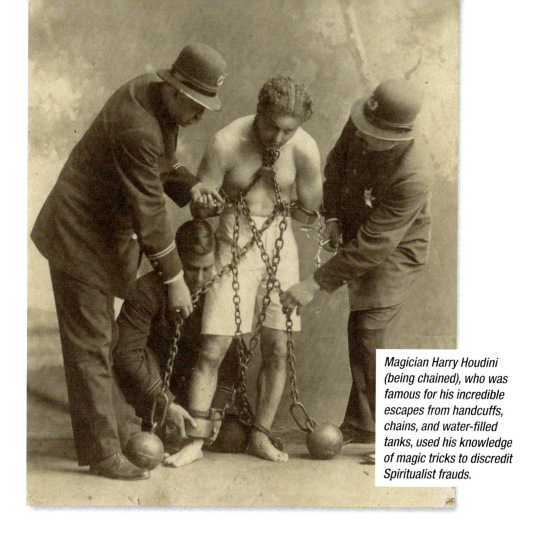

Magician Harry Houdini (being chained), who was famous for his incredible escapes from handcuffs, chains, and water-filled tanks, used his knowledge of magic tricks to discredit Spiritualist frauds.

in philosophy concerning paranormal activity and Spiritualism created a rift between Doyle and Houdini that remained for the rest of their lives.

Poltergeists and Parapsychology

Toward the end of the nineteenth century, as poltergeist-like activity in the Spiritualist world was captivating the public, it was also beginning to attract the attention of practitioners in a relatively new field of inquiry. Parapsychology, or the study of the mind's role in events not explainable through the standard sciences, arose as a response to Spiritualism's growing popularity. By 1889 parapsychologists were performing experiments designed to understand the causes of such psychic phenomena as clairvoyance (awareness of things beyond human senses), precognition (seeing the future), and telepathy (nonverbal communication between minds). Organizations dedicated to the study of parapsychology emerged, including the SPR in England in 1882, with a US branch, the American Society for Psychical Research, established three years later.

In 1930 Professor J.B. Rhine cofounded the Parapsychology Lab at Duke University in North Carolina. At the time, information on such psychic phenomena as poltergeist activity was generally gathered in the field by interviewing witnesses and victims of poltergeists. Rhine promoted parapsychology as an academic discipline that uses controlled laboratory experiments in addition to fieldwork to investigate psychic phenomena. His work included experiments in PK (the ability to move objects with the mind). His research involved rolling a pair of dice hundreds of times and recording their outcomes. Test subjects would try to influence each roll of the dice by mentally wishing for a total of eight or more. The dice were at first rolled by hand and later by a mechanical device to minimize human physical influence. The results of these experiments showed a greater than average outcome, suggesting that objects could be influenced with mind power alone. Skeptics soon began debunking Rhine's experiments. Author John Sladek writes, "Not only can dice be drilled, shaved, falsely numbered and manipulated, but even straight dice often show bias [due to manufacturing inconsistencies] in the long run."[30] Undaunted, Rhine continued his experiments in PK for the next three decades.

> "Not only can dice be drilled, shaved, falsely numbered and manipulated, but even straight dice often show bias [due to manufacturing inconsistencies] in the long run."[30]
>
> —Author John Sladek

Parapsychology and the Mind

Parapsychologist William G. Roll followed in Rhine's footsteps, joining Duke's Parapsychology Lab in 1957. Born in Germany

Ghost in a Box

One of the more elaborate tools used by ghost hunters and poltergeist investigators is a device called a ghost box. This handheld apparatus contains numerous electronic circuits that are claimed to facilitate communication with entities from the spirit world.

The idea behind the ghost box is that electronic voice phenomena, or voices from beyond, can be detected within the broadcast bands used by AM and FM radio. The device rapidly scans these frequencies, searching for sounds or voices in the spaces between broadcast stations. When the ghost box detects a word or phrase, it pauses the scan and records the audio for later analysis. Other functions include audio filters, adjustable scanning speeds, and a microphone for the investigator to talk to an entity.

Many users of ghost boxes report success in recording voices, and some say they can converse with an entity through the device. Others remain skeptical, attributing the results to misheard noises or wishful thinking. Perhaps more telling is the disclaimer by one manufacturer that its ghost box "does not guarantee . . . [capture of] any type of paranormal activity." So, let the (ghost hunting) buyer beware.

Quoted in Jennings Brown, "Proton Packs and Teddy Bears: The Pseudoscientific History of Ghost Hunting Gadgets," *Popular Mechanics*, October 26, 2016. www.popularmechanics.com.

---

in 1926, Roll studied psychology at the University of California, Berkeley, and then researched parapsychology at Oxford University in England, authoring numerous papers and books on psychic phenomena. Roll eventually earned a doctoral degree in psychology, based on his thesis, which was titled, "This World or That: An Examination of Parapsychological Findings Suggestive of the Survival of Human Personality After Death."

Beginning in 1958, Roll spent decades investigating poltergeist cases and authored numerous research papers examining the role of the brain in paranormal phenomena. His studies included the 1967 investigation of the poltergeist activity at the Tropication Arts warehouse in Miami, where he conducted controlled dice-throwing experiments with the main person of interest, shipping clerk Julio Vasquez. Roll became convinced that poltergeist activity was the result of PK.

As with Rhine and other paranormal investigators, Roll had his share of doubters. Despite criticism, however, Roll advocated increased study of psychic phenomena by researchers in scientific disciplines that studied the human mind:

> We have already seen the crucial role which psychologists, psychiatrists, and physical scientists have played in exploring the poltergeist. If research is to advance, it must continue to be interdisciplinary. . . . The exciting prospect which parapsychology has introduced is that this outer physical world and the inner psychical world may be one and the same.[31]

Ghost Hunters

The strict procedures and controls used in psychological testing for poltergeist activity might be seen as rather dull and academic. Not so are the exploits of the ghost hunters, who attempt to meet poltergeists on their own turf, armed with electronic gadgets to document their often-unnerving findings.

> "The exciting prospect which parapsychology has introduced is that this outer physical world and the inner psychical world may be one and the same."[31]
>
> —Parapsychologist William G. Roll

Poltergeists are nothing if not attention hounds. The flying furniture, eerie rapping sounds on walls, and disembodied voices lend themselves quite well to the modern-day ghost hunter, who is equipped with many tools to handle various aspects of the poltergeist phenomenon. Since spirit voices, often called electronic voice phenomena, are sometimes part of poltergeist activity, audio recorders are a primary part of the ghost hunter's tool kit. Digital technology has replaced analog tape in portable recorders, producing digital audio files that can be examined using audio software or emailed to specialized labs for analysis. In the 1964 Enfield poltergeist case, for example, hours of audio recordings of the entity's gruff voice were analyzed during the investigation.

Armed with electronics and other gadgets to document their findings, a group of ghost hunters prepares to meet poltergeists on their own turf.

Photos, Videos, and More

Cameras are also essential devices in the ghost hunter's toolbox to capture images of moving or levitating objects. Video and still cameras are among the most useful tools for documenting poltergeist activity. Sophisticated cameras from manufacturers such as Nikon and Canon can record stills, video, and audio with superior clarity, and they usually allow for better control over exposure, shutter speed, and time-lapse modes. Video of a chair or other object scooting untouched across a floor can be disconcerting, as can a still photo of a person floating in midair. But the possibility of faking a video or photo cannot be dismissed. Images can be cleverly manipulated either during shooting (a thin thread moving a chair can be invisible to the camera) or by using photo-editing software, which can often be downloaded for free.

Other useful poltergeist-hunting tools include the electromagnetic field (EMF) meter. In the everyday world, this device is a diagnostic tool designed to measure the EMF radiated from electrical devices, appliances, power lines, and even cell phones. According to ghost hunters, it can also detect the EMF allegedly emitted by spirit entities. There are also numerous ghost-hunting apps that adapt the functionality of many of these devices for cell phones. Not all tools are high tech. A simple digital thermometer can pinpoint cold spots often connected with poltergeists. Flashlights are useful not only for safety, but to illuminate possible poltergeist activity in a darkened space.

Whether any of these devices can actually detect evidence of paranormal activity is up for debate. Believers and skeptics obviously have their differences of opinion, and the controversy is not likely to be resolved anytime soon. So, the question remains: is it possible to definitively ascertain what poltergeists really are? There are many possibilities, and each one has its defenders and its detractors.

Poltergeists: Real or Unreal?

Joe Nickell is the senior research fellow of the international Committee for Skeptical Inquiry and a columnist for the organization's magazine, *Skeptical Inquirer*. As a former professional magician and private investigator, as well as having more than fifty years of experience in paranormal research, Nickell is well equipped to examine the authenticity of poltergeist activity. His reputation as a skeptic is notorious among paranormal investigators. Nickell pulls no punches in his opinions: "Those who promote belief in poltergeists often attribute the effects . . . to the repressed hostilities of a child or other person in the vicinity, which are somehow manifested as kinetic energy, supposedly a psychic force. Skeptics have a simpler explanation: they are the cunning pranks of a mischievous youth or disturbed adult."[32]

> "Those who promote belief in poltergeists often attribute the effects . . . to the repressed hostilities of a child or other person in the vicinity, which are somehow manifested as kinetic energy, supposedly a psychic force. Skeptics have a simpler explanation: they are the cunning pranks of a mischievous youth or disturbed adults."[32]
>
> —Skeptic Joe Nickell

Although Nickell says he has never encountered an authentic paranormal event in his years of investigation and research, he stresses the value of unbiased judgment, urging skeptics "not to be as closed-minded as the other side is ridiculously open-minded."[33] That other side, while not necessarily ridiculous, includes many parapsychologists, paranormal investigators, and others who believe that there is something out there that reason and logic cannot adequately explain.

So, the questions remain. What are poltergeists? Perhaps they are a sort of psychic phenomenon, or an event that has an obscure but natural explanation. They could be people misinterpreting certain normal happenstances. Alternatively, in many cases hoaxes and trickery cannot be ruled out. Theories abound, providing fuel for the discussion of what poltergeists are and how they manifest themselves in the world.

Poltergeist Hoaxes

The village of Amityville is a quiet, upscale residential community on the southern shore of Long Island, New York. For all its tranquil charm and popular beaches on Great South Bay, Amityville will always be remembered for the book and films known as *The Amityville Horror*. A tale of mass murder and terrifying paranormal occurrences, the story was at first touted as a factual account. But the truth turned out to be something quite different.

When George and Kathy Lutz purchased the house at 112 Ocean Avenue in Amityville in 1975, they were told of its violent history: in 1974, twenty-three-year-old Ronald DeFeo Jr. had murdered six family members in the house. Undaunted by this revelation, the Lutzes and their three children moved in on December 18, 1975. Strange things soon started to happen. A door was reportedly ripped off its hinges with no apparent cause; the house was uncomfortably cold, even with fires in the fireplace; a green, slimy substance appeared on the ceiling; and a priest summoned to bless the house reported a voice telling him to leave immediately. Less than a month after moving in, the Lutzes left, fleeing hurriedly and leaving their possessions behind.

What might have remained a local horror story became a national sensation with the publication of *The Amityville Horror* in 1977. The book became a best seller and was followed by movie

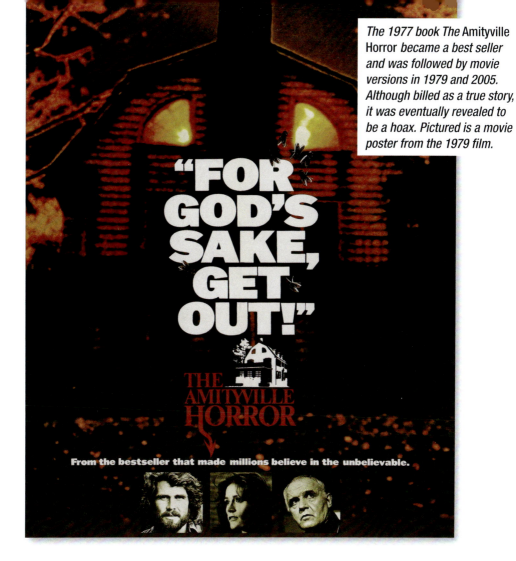

The 1977 book The Amityville Horror *became a best seller and was followed by movie versions in 1979 and 2005. Although billed as a true story, it was eventually revealed to be a hoax. Pictured is a movie poster from the 1979 film.*

versions in 1979 and 2005. Although billed as a true story, the book was eventually revealed to be a hoax. Parapsychologist Stephen Kaplan spent over two decades investigating the story. During that time, he found no evidence of paranormal activity. He also noted that there were many discrepancies within the original book, as well as details that had been altered in subsequent editions. In 1979 William Weber, who was DeFeo's lawyer, revealed that he and the Lutzes had made up the whole story. The couple had been in financial difficulty, which they hoped to ease with earnings from the book, and Weber was hoping for a new trial for DeFeo. "We created this horror story over many bottles of wine that George Lutz was drinking,"[34] Weber told an Associated Press reporter.

Philip the Artificial Poltergeist

During the 1970s a group of paranormal researchers created an artificial entity, a ghost of sorts, with whom they hoped to communicate. The group named their creation Philip and gave him a personal history. They imagined that Philip was a knight in seventeenth-century England who fought for the crown and became a secret agent for the English king. With Philip's backstory in place, the researchers conducted group sessions to try to contact their homemade entity. When they got no results, they began holding séances around a table and, according to members of the group, that is when things began to happen. The table vibrated and moved on its own, knocking noises were heard, and questions asked of Philip by the group were answered by coded rappings.

The group believed they had contacted a poltergeist of their own making. If an experiment like this one were to be done today, it probably would be accomplished with the help of artificial intelligence. And then, who knows what sort of communication might occur?

Poltergeist investigators can cite numerous cases involving trickery. For example, several mysterious house fires were blamed on poltergeists until investigations showed they were likely started by residents in the homes. Nickell describes such cases as examples of "poltergeist-faking syndrome."[35] A classic example of this occurred in 1984 in Columbus, Ohio, where poltergeist activity seemed to center on fourteen-year-old Tina Resch. The bizarre activity included a flying lamp, a shattered picture frame, and a famous photograph of a telephone zooming in midair in front of a seated Tina. Through video from television news crews on the scene, Tina was finally revealed to be the source of the strange goings-on. Cameras caught her setting up pranks when no one was looking. A teen with a troubled background, Tina apparently sought attention by faking the poltergeist activity.

Natural Explanations

Although attention seekers may fake poltergeist phenomena to impress, tease, or annoy others, they are not the only nonpsychic source of odd happenings. Ordinary forces of nature can play a part in creating poltergeist-like phenomena. For example, doors slamming shut are a commonly reported aspect of poltergeist events. If people are already experiencing odd events that they interpret as a poltergeist, a slamming door may reinforce their belief that it is the result of an unknown phenomenon. In that mindset, they may fail to realize that even a slight breeze can blow a door closed and instead attribute it to a paranormal source.

Physical vibrations may also cause poltergeist-like effects. Such vibrations may originate as underground tremors, subterranean flows of water, or the passing of heavy trucks and other vehicles on nearby highways. These may create cracks in walls or make pictures and other hanging objects swing or fall. Vibrations may also make windows rattle and cause lightweight furniture such as chairs, stools, or children's toys to move unaided across a floor. Vibroacoustical phenomena, or vibrations caused by sound waves, are another source sometimes attributed to poltergeists. One such incident involved an engineer who found that the metal rod he was working with began vibrating without any discernable cause. He also experienced chills, and the unnerving feeling that he was being watched, even though there was no one else in the lab. Although spooked, he set out to investigate.

Physical vibrations from heavy trucks and other traffic on nearby highways are cited as one explanation of poltergeist activity.

He discovered that the strange effects were the result of infrasound, a low-frequency sound below the human threshold of hearing that can induce vibrations. A new exhaust fan had recently been installed in the lab, and switching it off made the vibrations and physical uneasiness disappear.

Poltergeists and the Brain

Although the physical world has strange phenomena that can be used to explain poltergeist-like activity, it may turn out that the inner world of the human psyche can offer an even better explanation for perceived paranormal activity. The field of neuroscience is the study of the inner workings of the brain and nervous system. It combines many disciplines, including biology, physiology, psychology, and anatomy. According to *Psychology Today*, "Humans have an estimated hundred billion neurons, or brain cells, each with about a thousand connections to other cells."[36] This astonishing complexity explains why so much is still unknown about the human brain. The old saying that people only use 10 percent of their brain is wildly inaccurate: human beings use 100 percent, but scientists understand only about one-tenth of it. What lies within the other 90 percent could hold the key to countless mysteries, including poltergeists.

One example of the brain's ability to sense (or believers would say to create) unusual activity occurred during the COVID-19 pandemic. As the pandemic spread during 2020, the *New York Times* reported an upsurge in accounts of unexplained activity, including lights flickering, disembodied footsteps, and other noises—all of which are often attributed to poltergeists. The anxiety of being quarantined during the pandemic could have created mental stresses that led people to perceive sounds or lights or other events as poltergeist activity. Other sources of stress may include the illness or death of a loved one, a catastrophic incident such as a home destroyed by fire, or the breakup of a longtime relationship.

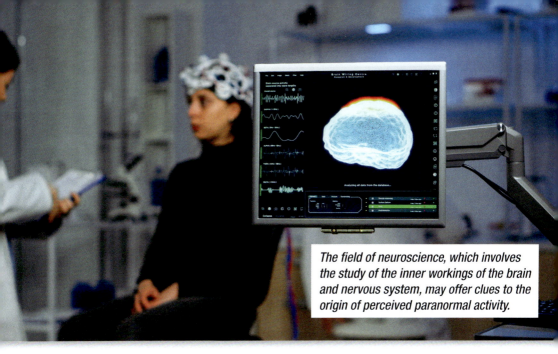

The field of neuroscience, which involves the study of the inner workings of the brain and nervous system, may offer clues to the origin of perceived paranormal activity.

Mind over Matter

William G. Roll spent years studying the human mind and exploring its complexities. But when he visited the home of the Herrmann family in Seaford, New York, in March 1958, he was not sure what to expect. For the past month the family had been alarmed by numerous bottles of liquids—shampoo, perfume, bleach, and other fluids—popping their tops and falling over, spilling their contents. This often happened when no one was nearby, but the sound of popping bottle caps usually alerted the family that something strange was taking place.

During a ten-day investigation of this phenomenon with his colleague Gaither Pratt, Roll speculated that the Herrmann's twelve-year-old son, Jimmy, might be mischievously causing the poltergeist activity. But Jimmy denied playing a prank and, given the obvious distress the family was experiencing, the investigators dismissed any thoughts of a hoax. Roll concluded that Jimmy was manipulating the bottles through PK.

Roll ultimately refined the definition of PK as it pertained to poltergeist activity like that in Miami, Seaford, and other incidents. He called it recurrent spontaneous psychokinesis (RSPK). The term refers to the phenomenon of PK when it is functioning without the

Proof of Poltergeists

Investigative journalist Michael Clarkson spent five years researching poltergeist phenomena. He has drawn some conclusions about paranormal researchers and the nature of poltergeist evidence:

> Most scientists will not accept eyewitness accounts or anecdotal evidence as proof that poltergeists exist. Why should they? People sometimes can be fooled, or can hallucinate.
>
> One piece of evidence that poltergeists exist is the fact that cases around the world share many common features (such as moving objects, rappings, and youthful agents), despite the fact that they are reported independently of each other.
>
> PK has been largely repudiated by the scientific community. However, Clarkson notes that one respected scientist believed that poltergeist activity is demonstrated by PK, the moving of objects with the mind. That scientist is the late Professor Robert Jahn, who was dean of the School of Engineering and Applied Sciences at Princeton University. Although it is difficult to research such phenomena due to the often-fleeting nature of psychic events, Jahn believed that substantial results had been provided by other researchers in the paranormal field.

Michael Clarkson, *The Poltergeist Phenomenon: An In-Depth Investigation into Floating Beds, Smashing Glass, and Other Unexplained Disturbances.* Pompton Plains, NJ: New Page, 2011, pp. 16–17.

---

conscious knowledge or direction of a person. It is recurrent—that is, it keeps happening over a period of time—and it is spontaneous because it occurs randomly without the person's deliberate control. These individuals have no knowledge that they are causing the disturbances and are as baffled by the incidents as those who witness them.

Mainstream scientists reject the notion of RSPK and are critical of Roll's research techniques. But among modern poltergeist researchers, the term *RSPK* has generally replaced the word *poltergeist*. Gathering evidence of RSPK can be difficult for investigators of poltergeist activity. Professor Robert Jahn founded and directed experiments in psychokinesis at the Princeton Engineering Anomalies Research Lab in New Jersey. Along with lab work in a controlled environment, fieldwork takes RSPK research to places where paranormal events occur. This can create unique problems in an area crowded with officials and curiosity seekers. An investigator, Jahn said, "typically finds the [poltergeist] site overrun by law enforcement officers, medical and psychological practitioners, the clergy, media, family members and skeptical representatives, who have so confounded and suppressed the effects that valid evidence is extremely difficult to obtain."[37] Yet such field investigations are important to create a complete picture of a poltergeist event.

Stories of poltergeists have been around for centuries, and the supernatural entities can be frightening, mildly disturbing, or simply amusing to those who encounter them. Depending on a person's belief system and world outlook, they can provide a glimpse of an existence beyond our corporeal realm, create a baffling psychic mystery, or present a prankster with an opportunity to play tricks on unsuspecting victims for laughs or to gain attention. Most paranormal researchers who have studied poltergeists now believe that the phenomenon reflects the inner world of the human brain rather than the external world of spooks and spirits. "Poltergeist phenomena," wrote Roll, "may not represent odd exceptions to the laws of nature, but lawful processes which have so far escaped our attention. If poltergeist phenomena say anything, I suspect that this is not about spirits, demons, or ghosts but about human personality."[38]

Ongoing paranormal research may eventually provide conclusive proof of the nature of poltergeists. In the meantime, books, movies, and television shows will continue to give us glimpses into the world of poltergeists, whether that world is found among the inner workings of the human mind or in a realm beyond human understanding.

> "[An investigator] typically finds the [poltergeist] site overrun by law enforcement officers, medical and psychological practitioners, the clergy, media, family members and skeptical representatives, who have so confounded and suppressed the effects that valid evidence is extremely difficult to obtain."[37]
>
> —Professor Robert Jahn, Princeton University

Introduction: Noisy Spirits

1. Al Cobb, *Danny's Bed: A Tale of Ghosts and Poltergeists in Savannah, Georgia*. Atglen, PA: Schiffer, 2007, p. 16.

Chapter One: Perturbed by Poltergeists

2. Quoted in *Daily Mail (London, UK)*, "Who You Gonna Call? Family Send in Paranormal Experts After 'Capturing Ghost' in Home Video," March 28, 2011. www.dailymail.co.uk.
3. John Fraser, *Poltergeist! A New Investigation into Destructive Hauntings*. Alresford, UK: Sixth, 2020, p. 2.
4. Quoted in Andrew Lang, *Cock Lane and Common-Sense*. London: Longmans, Green, 1894, p. 2.
5. Michael Clarkson, *Poltergeists: Examining Mysteries of the Paranormal*. Buffalo, NY: Firefly, 2005, p. 4.
6. Quoted in Alfred Owen Aldridge, "Franklin and the Ghostly Drummer of Tedworth," *William and Mary Quarterly*, vol. 7, no. 4, October 1950, pp. 559–67.
7. Claude Lecouteux, *The Secret History of Poltergeists and Haunted Houses: From Pagan Folklore to Modern Manifestations*. Rochester, VT: Inner Traditions, 2012, p. 15.
8. Quoted in Lecouteux, *The Secret History of Poltergeists and Haunted Houses*, p. 17.
9. Alan Gauld and A.D. Cornell, *Poltergeists*. London: Routledge & Kegan Paul, 1979, p. 231.

Chapter Two: Mischievous Poltergeists

10. Quoted in William G. Roll, *The Poltergeist*. New York: Paraview, 2004, p. 119.
11. Quoted in Roll, *The Poltergeist*, p. 169.
12. Quoted in Allen Spraggett, "Pursuing the Elusive Poltergeist," *Pittsburgh Press Roto*, January 6, 1974, p. 19.
13. Quoted in Spraggett, "Pursuing the Elusive Poltergeist," p. 19.
14. Quoted in BBC Radio 4, "The Reunion: What It's Like to Meet a Poltergeist," April 8, 2018. www.bbc.co.uk.
15. Quoted in Holly Evans, "Photographer Reveals Theory Behind Infamous Enfield Haunting 'Floating Child' Picture," *The Independent*, October 23, 2023. www.independent.co.uk.
16. Quoted in Clarkson, *Poltergeists*, p. 140.
17. Quoted in Clarkson, *Poltergeists*, p. 140.

Chapter Three: Dangerous Poltergeists

18. Quoted in Tori Jane, "A 1940s Indiana Home Once Had 28 Fires Set in One Day by an Unseen Force and It Was Never Explained," Only in Your State, December 4, 2020. www.onlyinyourstate.com.

19. Quoted in Richard Moreno, *Myths and Mysteries of Illinois: True Stories of the Unsolved and Unexplained.* Guilford, CT: Globe Pequot, 2013, p. 32.
20. Quoted in Moreno, *Myths and Mysteries of Illinois*, p. 38.
21. Quoted in Vincent H. Gaddis, *Mysterious Fires and Lights*. New York: David McKay, 1967, p. 198.
22. Darren W. Ritson, *The South Shields Poltergeist: One Family's Fight Against an Invisible Intruder*. Cheltenham, UK: History, 2020, p. 78.
23. Quoted in Ritson, *The South Shields Poltergeist*, p. 194.
24. Quoted in Darren W. Ritson, "The South Shields Poltergeist, 15 Years On," Spooky Isles, May 28, 2021. www.spookyisles.com.
25. Quoted in Jonathan Brown, "'Haunted' Semi-detached Yorkshire House at Centre of *Live Most Haunted* Halloween TV Special," *Yorkshire Evening Post,* October 31, 2015. www.yorkshireeveningpost.co.uk.
26. Quoted in Brown, "'Haunted' Semi-detached Yorkshire House at Centre of *Live Most Haunted* Halloween TV Special."
27. Quoted in Brown, "'Haunted' Semi-detached Yorkshire House at Centre of Live *Most Haunted* Halloween TV Special."

Chapter Four: Seeking the Truth

28. Quoted in Alice Askins, "Very Mysterious: The Fox Sisters and the Spiritualist Movement," Historic Geneva, September 29, 2017. www.historicgeneva.org.
29. Quoted in Casey Cep, "Why Did So Many Victorians Try to Speak with the Dead?," *New Yorker,* May 24, 2021. www.newyorker.com.
30. John Sladek, *The New Apocrypha: A Guide to Strange Sciences and Occult Beliefs*. New York: Stein and Day, 1973, p. 174.
31. Roll, *The Poltergeist*, p.198.

Chapter Five: Poltergeists: Real or Unreal?

32. Joe Nickell, "Firebug Poltergeists," *Skeptical Inquirer,* January/February 2020. www.skepticalinquirer.org.
33. Joe Nickell, "The New Idolatry," *Point of Inquiry* (podcast), September 28, 2007. www.pointofinquiry.org.
34. Quoted in Joe Nickell, "Amityville: The Horror of It All," *Skeptical Inquirer,* January/February 2003, p. 14.
35. Joe Nickell, "Solving the 1932 Bladenboro Fire-Poltergeist Case," *Investigative Briefs* (blog), Center for Inquiry, January 26, 2016. www.centerforinquiry.org.
36. *Psychology Today*, "What Is Neuroscience?," November 16, 2009. www.psychologytoday.com.
37. Quoted in Clarkson, *Poltergeists,* p. 205.
38. Roll, *The Poltergeist*, p. 12.

Books

John Fraser, *Poltergeist! A New Investigation into Destructive Hauntings*. Alresford, Hampshire, UK: Sixth, 2020.

Marc Hartzman, *Chasing Ghosts: A Tour of Our Fascination with Spirits and the Supernatural*. Philadelphia: Quirk, 2021.

Bryan Laythe et al., *Ghosted! Exploring the Haunting Reality of Paranormal Encounters*. Jefferson, NC: McFarland, 2022.

Kate Summerscale, *The Haunting of Alma Fielding: A True Ghost Story*. New York: Penguin, 2021.

Internet Sources

Alan Boyle, "10 Terrifying Tales of Violent Poltergeists," Listverse, March 10, 2014. www.listverse.com.

Jennings Brown, "Proton Packs and Teddy Bears: The Pseudoscientific History of Ghost Hunting Gadgets," *Popular Mechanics*, October 26, 2016. www.popularmechanics.com.

Neil Dagnall and Kenneth Drinkwater, "Eight Things You Need to Know About Poltergeists—Just in Time for Halloween," The Conversation, October 26, 2017. www.the conversation.com.

How It Works, "Victorian Seances: The Ingenious Tricks Used to 'Speak to the Dead,'" July 3, 2016. www.howitworksdaily.com.

Joe Nickell, "Firebug Poltergeists," *Skeptical Inquirer*, January/February 2020. www.skepticalinquirer.org.

Neely Tucker, "Hollywood, Houdini and the Halloween Seance of 1936," *Timeless* (blog), Library of Congress, October 30, 2020. https://blogs.loc.gov.

Websites

Committee for Skeptical Inquiry (CSI)
www.skepticalinquirer.org
The CSI is a program within the nonprofit organization Center for Inquiry. It takes a scientific and skeptical approach to the paranormal, including poltergeists. Its publication, *Skeptical Inquirer,* reports on investigations of ghosts and other phenomena.

Occult World
www.occult-world.com

This website contains information on all types of strange phenomena, including cryptozoology, demons, witchcraft, and ghosts. The poltergeist section contains in-depth information on such famous cases as Enfield, Miami, and Seaford, as well as many other less well-known incidents.

Society for Psychical Research (SPR)
www.spr.ac.uk

This is the website for the oldest organization using scientific principles to investigate paranormal activity. It contains information on current research projects, notes for paranormal investigators, an online encyclopedia of the paranormal, and access to back issues of the *Magazine of the Society for Psychical Research*.

Note: Boldface page numbers indicate illustrations.

Adam, Sigmund, 21, 22
Age of Enlightenment, 12
Aldridge, Alfred Owen, 10
American Society for Psychical Research, 44
Amityville Horror, The (book, film), 50–51, **51**
Andrews family, 38–39

Bender, Hans, 22–23
Brooks, Howard, 19
Buntin, Sinclair, 19
Burgard, John, 31

Center for Scientific Inquiry, 7
clairvoyance, 44
Clarkson, Michael, 10, 56
Cobb family (Al, Jason), 5–6, 14
Committee for Skeptical Inquiry (CSI), 24, 49, 60
Conjuring 2, The (film), 35
Cornell, A.D., 15, 16
COVID-19 pandemic, 54

DeFeo, Ronald, Jr., 50, 51
Deism, 12
Doyle, Arthur Conan, 42–43

electromagnetic field (EMF) meters, 47–48
Enfield (UK) poltergeist, 23–27, 35

Ferreira, Maria José, 32
Fielding, Yvette, 36, 37
Fox sisters (Maggie, Kate, and Leah), **39**, 39–40, 41

Franklin, Benjamin, 10
Fraser, John, 8

Gauld, Alan, 15, 16
ghost boxes, 45
ghost hunters, 46, **47**
  tools used by, 47–48
Ghost Research Society, 24
Grosse, Maurice, 25–27, **26**

Hackler family, 28–30
Hagemeyer, Curt, 18
Herrmann family, 55
History of Spiritualism, The (Doyle), 42
Hodgson family, 24–27
Houdini, Bess, 41
Houdini, Harry, 41, 42–43, **43**

Jaboticabal (Brazil) poltergeist, 32
Jahn, Robert, 56–57
Johnson, Jan, 21

Kaplan, Stephen, 51
Karlsonn, Marc, 33, 34–35, 36
Killin, William, 19

Laubheim, Alvin, 18, 19
Lecouteux, Claude, 11
Luther, Martin, 12, 14
Lutz family, 50

Macomb (IL) poltergeist, 30–33
Magician Among the Spirits, A (Houdini), 42
Manning, Elle, 8
Manning, Lisa, 8, 9
McNeil family, 30–33
Mompesson, John, 10

Morris, Graham, 25
Most Haunted Live (TV program), 36

neuroscience, 54, 55
New York Times (newspaper), 54
Nickell, Joe, 24, 49–50, 52
Nottingham, Gary, 25
Nottingham, Vic, 25

Occult World, 61

paranormal, organizations researching, 24, 44
parapsychology, 43
Pennsylvania Gazette (newspaper), 10
Peterworth, Marianne, 33, 35
Peterworth, Robert, 33, 35
Playfair, Guy Lyon, 26
Poltergeist (film), 35
poltergeist(s), **16**
　activities related to, 15–16, 46
　agents for, 8
　definition of, 8–9
　as the devil's work, 14
　in history, 10
　malevolent, 28–37
　natural explanations for, 52–54
　nature of evidence for, 56
　origin of term, 6
　people's familiarity with, 11
　stages of activity, 13–15
　theories about, 7
　view of medieval Christian church on, 11–12
Pontefract (UK) poltergeist, 36–37
Pratt, Gaither, 20, 55
precognition, 44
Pritchard family, 36–37
psychokinesis (PK), 23, 44
　recurrent spontaneous, 55–57
Psychology Today (magazine), 54

recurrent spontaneous psychokinesis (RSPK), 55–57
Resch, Tina, 52
Rhine, J.B., 44, 46
Ritson, Darren, 34
Roll, William G., 20, 44–46, 55, 57
Rosenheim (Germany), **22**
　poltergeist haunting in, 20–23

Schaberl, Annemarie, 21, 23
Schroeder, Sophie, 32–33
Seaford poltergeist, 35
séances, 12–13, **13**, 40–41
Secret History of Poltergeists and Haunted Houses, The (Lecouteux), 11
Skeptical Inquirer (magazine), 49
Sladek, John, 44
Smith, Susy, 19
Society for Psychical Research (SPR), 7, 24, 61
South Shields (UK) poltergeist, 33–36
Spiritualist movement, 12, 40
　revival in 1920s, 42
surveys, on belief in spirits/spirit world, **4**

Table Talk (Luther), 14
telepathy, 44
"This World or That" (Roll), 45
Toys "R" Us haunting (Sunnyvale, CA), 21
Tropication Arts haunting (FL), 18–20, 45

Vasquez, Julio, 18, 20, 45

Weber, William, 51
Willey family, 31–33
Wilson, Fred, 31

Yorkshire Evening Post (newspaper), 36–37

PICTURE CREDITS

Cover: Joeprachatree/Shutterstock

4: Maury Aaseng
7: Serghei Starus/Shutterstock
9: Darren Baker/Shutterstock
13: Chronicle/Alamy Stock Photo
16: Alta Oosthuizen/Shutterstock
19: Tapati Rinchumrus/Shutterstock
22: FooTToo/Shutterstock
26: Trinity Mirror/Mirrorpix/Alamy Stock Photo
30: Mike Devlin/Science Source
34: Yhelfman/Shutterstock
36: Yorkshire Pics/Alamy Stock Photo
39: Chroma Collection/Alamy Stock Photo
43: Vintage_Space/Alamy Stock Photo
47: KinoMasterskaya/Shutterstock
51: Avalon/ZUMA Press/Newscom
53: JW.photography31/Shutterstock
55: DC Studio

ABOUT THE AUTHOR

Craig E. Blohm has written numerous books and magazine articles for young readers. He and his wife, Desiree, reside in Tinley Park, Illinois.